CICADA, DOG, & SONG

Cicada, Dog, & Song

Poems

Matt Thomas

Cicada, Dog, & Song

Copyright © 2026 Matt Thomas
First Edition

Paperback ISBN: 9781947175808

All rights reserved. No part of this book may be reproduced or transmitted in any form or by any means, electronic, digital, or mechanical, including photocopy, audio recording, or any information storage and retrieval system, without prior permission from the publisher or author (except by reviewers who may quote brief passages). No part of this book may be used or reproduced in any manner for the purpose of training artificial intelligence technologies or systems.

Front cover art: Amelia Mangham

Author photo: Michelle Thomas

Cover design by Jacob Arms
Published by Broken Tribe Press
Lawrence Landing Company
Raleigh, North Carolina 27609
USA, North America

Serving House Books is a proud member of:

Independent Book Publishers Association
 and
Community of Literary Magazines and Presses

www.servinghousebooks.com

For Michelle and Autumn

CONTENTS

Elephants	1

CICADA

First Responder	3
Seep	5
Cycle	6
Gift	7
Apple Jacks	8
Drought	9
Deadfall	11
At the Kennedy	12
The Climb	13
Isometrics	14
Billy's Boy	15
Diapause	17
The Mechanic	18
Jack Sprat	20
Pall Bearer	21
Black Walnut	22
Parable of the Sower	23
Reps	25
Sock	27
Brethren	28
The Story of Our Labor	29

DOG

People Watching	33
Moriah	34
Days	36

The Recruit	37
Wall Dancers	38
Slug	40
The Climate Conversation	41
Anniversary Poem III	43
The Birthday Poem	44
An Empathy	46
Cow Creek	47
An Epiphany	48
Lords of Appetite	49
Boys Life	50
Imposter Syndrome	51
Game Trail	53
Anthropomorphism	54
Roosevelt Island	55
Clout Dogs	56
Partners	58
Belt	59
Poem that Fails to Explain...	60
Rest Stop	62
Yet, the Dogs	63
Listening to Brian Wilson...	64

SONG

King of the Road	67
The Art Thief	69
Tasseography	70
Clovis	71
The Evidence Suggests	72
Psalm	73

Fire Drill	74
Low Water	75
Please Share	76
Trash	77
Let Me Be There	78
Enucleation	79
Bees	80
Urinal Poem	81
Hillbilly	83
Towel	84
Commuter Culture	85
The Third Law of Motivation	86
Anniversary Poem II	87
Consider the Day	88
Acknowledgements	91
About the Author	

"Le moutonnement des hais / C'est en moi que je l'ai"

The woolly hedges / I keep inside me

—Jean Wahl, *Poemes*

Elephants
borrowing a line from Emily Dickinson

A sun catcher
limiting the spectrum
to a few colors
when the pale stripe on the carpet
holds them all

The macrame elephant in the room

ear to my clicking, scraping
needles louder than the obvious,
feeding the world, teaching it tricks
unwilling to believe
that each thing is equal
to its naked light

And with a Blonde push

a totem is chosen. Once selected it can't be undone, cemented every gift giving holiday, confirmed by collection during each visit to your bedroom until it is a daemon accompanying you into adulthood, clinging like all assumed inevitabilities such as a once honest delight in your own imagination, a fantastic animal as proof of nature's promise to amuse, surprise, extended even to yourself now set, rigid, staring wherever its fixed eyes are pointed, projecting sun in a way you've learned to expect, were taught to dissect but aren't elephants wise, members of close-knit communities, fierce and clever creatures? So your spirit on some unplumbed level must describe those characteristics you think watching the dust filter down from where you've stirred it considering your possibilities, your elephants.

Cicada

First Responder

There's the pile of stuff
and then the other
not beneath
or in any dimensional space

The weight

of autobiography,
sop of what you've taken to heart,
stray hair bookmarking the page,
flakes of skin in the gutter

As soon as the lesson is learned
it's a rock littering the side of the road
next to the Watch for Falling Rock sign
sighing on its springs,
shying from traffic:
the kind of empathy
that dreams sitting on its luggage

Memory and imagination

the problem of description, prayer
dense as a black hole
signaling to the universe

Tap, tap, tap

of the catbird

with your child's ribbon,
pennant of a forgotten Easter,
perched in the cedar:

how we are taught
to reach out to the other side.

Seep

Standing waiting on a dog
to lift a leg, squat,
holding the leash wearing
what could only be described as
hurried dress, pajamas or
something pulled from the laundry
smelling of yesterday
or the day before

Maybe in a light rain
no coat, or slippered in the snow
praying that this similar mammal
might get the message
so that I can return
to warmth under roof in the way
that I had imagined
when I first saw the puppy

as curled at my feet, trusted;
the long exposed topmost
of what takes years to surface
All that I seem to have sight for

the greater percentage of my living
has never tasted air, seen light

and this dog, these elements
are the seep, the evidence
I confuse with mystery

Cycle

Cicada fretting the lack of time

Dog digging
to get something or leave it I don't know

Same day as night, nothing changes but seeing
In sun, green carapace / moon, white belly

Song, ticking
an overwatch, eyes / on the cycling seasons

Gift

A wooden glider,
propeller wound
with a rubber band

and a new word, 'balsa'
Better than the bikes,
cowboy boots and cap guns.

Bought at a truck stop,
a last minute gift,
handed to me distracted
with homecoming

A fraction heavier than nothing
It's a dream of what?
A whiskered skull

rubbing my knuckles,
offered,
a little balsa plane.

Apple Jacks

The moon isn't a fingernail
it's a dark planet,
falling around the earth forever.
You aren't my other half
we are animals,
bearing closed cultures.
Wife, month:
borrowed words
taking up everlasting slack.
You,
sitting in the kitchen
with a box of Apple Jacks.
The moon,
posted dutifully outside.
Sticks and a stone,
charged by wooly cold,
repelling names,
asking in whispers into
the necks of each other
for a missing measure
of balance. Willing
the days to lengthen,
crazy to return to opposite shifts,
escape the cling
of cellmates up all night
at the kitchen table
speaking the painfully exact
language of distance.

Drought

Headlights bob in the road particulate
hunting day for night
same as I'm sitting beneath prop cloud cover
imagining rain that smells like black currant
while drought dampens sound and sharpens light,
curls the day like paper birch, agitates
a wasp crisscrossing
the empty mouth of a rain barrel
in a silent, electric expression
of unfulfilled passion

like that of the standup piano sitting
in a small trailer in the driveway across the street,
warping, sucking wind, surrounded
by jagged odd lengths of PVC pipe,
a broken wicker chair.
Given up, waiting
for the clang and jolt of the hitch
to be rendered out of and away
from the geography of its purpose, jealous
of the coffee phlegm'd Spanish of sons
who don't play
cleaning up the aftermath
of a father's unexpected death
resonating across the road to me
in my artificial shade,
a lilt and cough longing for things to be ordered
once again according to what was:
music in the barrel

sounding an ever-deepening note,
each endangered native thing
brought back into tune and place,
a found Middle C,
the filigreed shadow of creeper in a sun
gentle enough to entertain

Deadfall

It crashes like a tree
but is probably a branch
on a still Sunday morning,
stiller for the humidity,
lack of air

Immediately I create
a story, how it split
after many years under weight,
fell in a tangle
to the leaves below

I can see it happening
and now it has, just that way
become a fact
I'll remember years later
suddenly with a similar
crack and rush

At the Kennedy
For Julien Baker

When a teacher demonstrated a tuning fork
I thought, ah
to conduct
the pitch and letter of each tense ...

In '78 no one cared how far out I floated
asleep rafting the Atlantic
while my family said and did
whatever I couldn't hear or see

I learned to resonate
by sprawled length and mass
my own constant tone, struck
on the realization that strangeness swells
beneath the familiar, so that now
when the symphony surges and breaks
I close my eyes
and wait for the pull,

facedown on the rough seams of my day,
not seizing, another thing a teacher said,
but prone,
fingers in the twitch
feeling
for the unfathomable, alien heart.

The Climb

A little green worm climbing my beer can.
To look at him is to feel the bones
sleeved by your right arm
once bent into a perfect U by a fall,
healed arrow straight although
there are two dimples
where the screws were removed
that we call your 'shark bite.'
He summits, takes in the view,
hangs on through a gust
that skitters the can
an inch across the table,
and then curls away and down,
facing his descent.
From what?
He seems satisfied
with the empty exercise,
more so than me, drinking
in the narrow alley
between work days.

What we need, I think
is for someone to break something,
taste giddy awe again beneath
the humility of a mistake.

Isometrics

Mrs. S was from Upper Darby and sounded like it, a toothy combination of wise acre and affable distrust in an olive touched indoor skin, eyes black in the way that a white horse is called gray. She had no argument with existing, unlike my Fundamentalist family, and free of that selfish piety was generous: she tolerated my strangeness; she bantered sweetly with my awkward imp, feeding it within bounds; I felt almost normal, like a boy without answers. She planted tulips in mulched beds by the ground level windows. Her husband mowed the grass every two weeks, a salesman's car-bound, boozy build. "He's going to have a stroke," my parents laughed. When the summer humidity became too much we kids lounged around her basement, read *Thrasher*, watched the VCR. We were 'morons,' 'shits,' 'monkeys;' all the things I knew myself to be but was never allowed at my own house. Her exuberant, pretended irritation loosed the tourniquet of my enforced alienation, made me confidant to a broader humanity. While visiting I never asked anything of the mirror, was figurative only in a derivative sense, learning to carry my body, my literal weight. Walking back evenings across the yards to certainty I mooned after confusion, flexed temerity in the dusk gelled bugs and whip-poor-wills and distant barking dogs until I worked myself into the conviction that the world would take me back after abandoning it, the glowing toes of my high tops the dashed white lines of that empty, begged stretch.

Billy's Boy
For Autumn

Summers so hot the wood pulp smelled like blood
retread tires bulging at the weight,
front high and light, steering
like an aunt's kiss,
cloud of blue following the truck
same as the saw.
Billy's boy,
tired, wishing
miles to the trip not worried
about the dry rot that hunches Billy over the wheel,
gloves beside him on the bench
curled into the shape of his hands.

I didn't know what to do with you at first.
If a thing was in the room with me
I was too shy to see it. I had to wait
for the flattening wake to enjoy in passing
its sweet dimming galaxy of bioluminescence.

I had a hard time with reality.
Big events floored me.
I knew what I wanted,
but I had to learn to love everything,
a fog to myself, doing to be.

It took decades to learn the trick
of sponging the moment,
no hard craft, only water and reach.

It wasn't you or your mom that brought me around,
nor me. I just woke to it
same as Billy's hand
on my flannelled shoulder,
"hey guy, we're home."

Diapause

We are cleaved to each other, what was said
at the promise, married
to the advantage
of bilateral symmetry
Yet we pause, periodically
separating at some intuition
of seasonal poverty
to awkwardly stretch limbs
that had been tucked inside the other,
atrophied, painfully stiff but
gradually greased and muscled
by necessity rediscovered
until plenty folds us once again
into seamed hemispheres,
the knot of scar a heart,
sense organ of our partnership
evolving sunder to sunder
into what God has joined.

The Mechanic

How is sleep different than death?
Every night I count backwards, begging,
never thinking of the afterlife of morning.

When I was young I babysat
three descending sisters
with beautiful golden hair, camping
their Barbies in a pink RV
while our mothers drank coffee
until their father,
a round-faced pleasant man,
hung himself in the garage.

I was alive with those three little girls, and young,
as was my mother and their parents.
We all have a 100% chance of making it
from the beginning of that memory to the end.

If I give up on sleep and walk the dogs outside
the door will open to the things
not allowed into the house
like the Corona Borealis, ground crickets,
and a breeze that carries
beneath fox musk and coal smoke
the lingering belch of countless bodies producing
mechanical energy, a tongue to battery, tooth
to tinfoil salivation inducing sense
of a power unlikely to suffer imbalance,
come apart at the vibration of life.

That stink is my hallelujah, not
the stunning beauty of the ridges rising black
as the moon sets or the singing bare
branches of the trees rubbing in gusts
but numbering the parts because
what works can be taken apart and regarded
the way that prayer disassembles,
arranges a life in cleaned and oiled pieces

and maybe then, reminded that it's matter,

not the lubricating spirit
lingering on my hands that I love,
I can return inside,
feed the dogs, pull a blanket over us on the couch
and joyfully, finally, die.

Jack Sprat
For my father

Trimming chops for dinner
working a thin knife
behind rubbery squid-white
carefully so as not to waste meat
peeling elastin
into a ginger-like mound on the plate
that plays with the light
while I consider a nursery rhyme
recited often by my father
about Jack Sprat and his wife,
and the possible happy compatibility
of unbridgeable,
fundamental difference
leagued to clean a plate.
Which when you think about it
is the kind of ingenious flexibility
to which partnership aspires,
maintaining shape and connection
in lean times and fat,
handling likes and dislikes
with the skill required
to leave well enough alone.

Pall Bearer
For Leroy

A refrigerator
I once helped him
Navigate into the basement
An awkward weight
Now his

Hush the baby

All the boys came
Left their dozers and backhoes
To say goodbye,
Think for a moment heavy thoughts
Then climb back into trucks,
Turn on radios to spite the quiet.

Black Walnut

Pratfall, food, seed ...
what better description of anything,
everything, I think,
sitting in deer tick infested grass
holding an ankle rolled
on a black walnut.

Parable of the Sower

Two trees with bad roots
Planted by Lamont, dead six years now
He'd have replaced them had we told him
But we watched each stunt in their individual ways,
waiting for them to figure it out
We couldn't know that they didn't have means

This morning I cut them down
17 years of trying
Just a quick crescendo of throttle
And they fell to bounce
softly on their boughs
the way that evergreens do,
pinecones like little bells on the ground

We built this house at the turn of the Century
when we were thirty,
and had been not-poor long enough
to dare to believe ourselves rich

Before we arrived
the neighbors courted in our woods,
walking deer trails yet unbroken by a house
For a while they told us that story
every time they saw us
Now they're moved away
and we tell the story

The turn of the Century seems
a ridiculous thing to remember.
100 years, a random unit
to house our lives, most of which
are spent outside trespassing
undeveloped romance,
swinging hands
with a husband's conceit

Reps

Products on the edge of a hotel tub brought packaged according to TSA regulations and against spills, pressure bursting, freezing at altitude, etc. Moisturizers, under eye cream, shampoos, conditioners. Containing octopus ink, kale, charcoal, seaweed. Tea infused, ionized but no sulfates, parabens, phthalates. Bearing the Leaping Bunny Logo, internationally recognized symbol guaranteeing a product has not been tested on animals. Masked on my face, smeared on my arms, hands, and neck. Massaged into my sags, scars, tells of having continued to wake up years past a lot of other people so that I might sit on a toilet at a Hilton in Arizona counting focus-group tested shapes self-soothing itinerary anxieties such as directions, estimated travel times, reservations, hours of operation. 1,2,3,4, reaching the end and returning to 1, a habit acquired by a lifetime of daily repetitious exercises counted off to balanced form, a pat on the back from the mirror, subtle positive evaluations from partners, strangers; signs of the cross made with manicured middle fingers at death. Which despite the common comfort of ordering is a dependable chaos that has occurred famously in exactly this position, tired boxers frowning beneath ashy knees, no heart, guts for an arid climate and cowboy steak. Slumped in the inevitable Least Attractive Pose while a housekeeper dials 911 on speaker contemplating a screen saver of her kids thinking of the story she'll have for her sister, reciting the facts of the matter to the operator in the stink of my last earthly contribution, calming herself by counting my many bottles and jars, reducing risk of panic; a measure of efficacy and a kind of statistical beauty, or at least a positive return on investment, which, as balance and margin, may be all that anyone on either side of the deal can ask.

Sock

Clothes in the cinders
and weeds alongside the road ...
as kids we'd pick them up with sticks, fling them,
soggy with what we assumed was sex,
at each other hooting and running
from the flailing thing
dangerous with having been discarded
intentionally in a purposeless land:
the dimly lit, sick country
of the un-wheeled adult,
afoot sad stories hazarding waylay
by bad luck and violence

How and why a proof of travel had come to rest
in clouds of carbon monoxide
and rushing steel doing violence to the air
was the kind of question
we thought more necessary than food
to becoming an adult,
rummaging anything wrong-minded
for proof that our mother's voices,
calling us home to tables, were unwell, not right.

Brethren

You brought a ball and glove,
Possessed of the romantic notion
that the two of you would picnic, play
as if at a family gathering, 4th of July maybe,
like older cousins introducing their girlfriends,
not the spit and skin taste of kicking around
an empty church camp ball diamond,
outfield grass gone red and to seed, leaves
fleeing the evening, waiting
for sign of an unspoken agreement
to consume a mutual notion,
walk a dirt path to jimmy a door
stepping carefully on the way
over the fat aerial roots of towering Oaks,
your show of rubbing hands, arms,
a gesture not so much for warmth
as mockery of ritual,
although you refused to disbelieve,
hot and flustered
in the small, invaded cabin watching another
for the first time
wash your feet, dry them with their hair.

The Story of Our Labor

We learned to weave, braid
what we had woven, practiced
the known knots so
that on the day when deftness woke
us we were able to fasten
what we knew and climb
ourselves up and out of our many rooms

We built ladders, suspension bridges,
nets for sleeping or falling,
ruined our thumbs on the work
monkeying that time
feeling finally free and able
eating the yolks of each broken day and when
we realized no more desire
our daughter
set about picking the knots,
reverse engineering
the heart we had invented,
until our structures became ropes
and the ropes became strings,
the strings became fibers
and the fibers became twist and thread

in a heap carted to the parts stash,
the how-to in reserve, palleted, waiting
for the day it occurred to her to sew
the things she had been tearing,
which was new and exciting
for a time and then, holding a thread,
she thought to twist it until it became a rope,
and then to tie this piece to that

Dog

People Watching

Driving black ice on a river road
in a cathedral of moon shadow
on snow beneath cedars
trying to remember
what you ordered for lunch
at my elbow watching the Square
from our usual window seat.

A jogger ran past, ear gauges like portholes
framing a glimpse of boarding school kids
laughing with their laundry:

cold sky, evergreens, dirty snow,
mint copper roof of the Gazebo,
backpack hampers and high tops
in bouncing flesh circles

and you removed the lettuce
from what I want to say
was half an avocado BLT
but I'm only guessing, rueful, feeling for a loss
of traction knowing
that someday I will need the care I've taken
and goddamn me
for looting anything but you.

Moriah

- the name given to a mountainous region in the Book of Genesis, where the binding of Isaac by Abraham is said to have taken place

for your mother

She walked as if pushed from behind,
red corduroys faded to orange,
yellow ski jacket,
all of her in my mind soft, even
the bones of her elbows sleeved in down
exiting the 7-11 following a State Trooper
to your grandmother's Ford,
where you watched from a car seat
impatient for that softness.

Their footsteps crunched in the snow
just beneath the radio
until the door opened,
her gym class Keds dirty in the slush
beside and behind his lug soled boots
while he leaned into the car,
his breath pushing ahead
like another face, fat and round
asking "Are you OK?"
And at your nod,
starch and sweat lingering,
(which from then on will be the smell of cold)
turned to say, not ask,
shawled in curling exhaust,

"What kind of mother..."

A statement you breathed
back at her on the way home restless
with validation,
her auburn hair shaking below
a pilled knit cap as she drove crying,
remembering the threat:
Child Protective Services,
as if there were such a thing,
while you tongued your adult teeth,
over large in your mouth,
like the new taste of her blood
not quite good
that you acquired considering
the ways you had been slighted and would be,
righteousness running
like a dog beside the car.

A scene I composed forty years ago
as my mother told me the story
and my heart ached for myself
not yet taken to Moriah
but knowing it was a matter of time
as she gushed about you,
the sweet rope and knife
in the back of your grandmother's car.

Days

There are days
that taste like silt
and smell like sucker fish
and those that are pink and green,
rise and set like a bite.

Sometimes a day ends with the sound
of cut wood tonked onto a pile
others a squeal and clang
as if under construction.

I thought last night,
'The bug flecked bulb,'
watching birds traverse the moon,
a bitterly cold day as always yet
as always sounding
like thaw.

The Recruit

One of those first discovered
self-conscious words

corps,

on a poster in my room,
The Few, The Proud,
dress blues, swords erect
implying charges
over banked corpses

companions of the kiss of the earth,
and of my quickening man
which would rather lie
in the grass sighing
descriptions for things,

like the pinhole projector crescent
of a cowlick'd sun asking for a smudge,
or an ant making the signs of itself,

than cross the road
to contemplate a given name,
dare that high, weird feeling
of empty asphalt,
speeding tonnage around the bend,

the smooth, baking firmament
beneath Chuck Taylors

slapping forward to glimpse
the kinds of bodies I could be.

Wall Dancers

We called them wall dancers,
the people who locked eyes
with the concrete
and followed the movements
of the light washed there, dancing
by themselves,
an internal shyness
like sun teething at clouds
as we moved around them,
parting, a school
of bunched and darting jealousies,
grudges, open and secret
romances worn like club clothes
while they, self-contained
dared their shadow to follow,
advance and retreat
the way that canopies of trees pas de deux,
or fighting cocks meet mid air
undulating energy,
the language of ebb and flow reminding me
that alone in my bedroom
I had once been a student of my life,
the thump and climb of the BeeGees
gently collapsing one joint
and standing another
asking why I was not interested
in more fully occupying my space

something I'd remember later
tired and hung over
the edge of being
one of many,
those mornings where the longing
to hold myself closely and apart
was most acute.

Slug

Delicately spun
glossy chocolate trumpets

Extended
as much a face as mine

But wary now, withdrawn,
personality put away

An easily won release
from my attention

Boredom - its
defense - my fear

The Climate Conversation

It used to be summer that had no confidence,
mind of baby fat,
but now it's hard as a slap,
forgotten all about
the days it used to wake damp,
shuffle smelly feet to the kitchen
wait for coffee while
playing with rabbit chewed hair

I told someone once,
before I knew to keep my losses to myself,
on the way back to a party
from a run to the liquor store,
that I could hear every disappointment
of every person in the world,
living or dead

blurted out
in one of those earnest boozy conversations
I used to have with people who
had no similar need

Now, when winter leans
back to take a weak lukewarm piss,
cigarette dangling from slack fingers,
complaining about the voices
of eroding beaches, calving glaciers,

tennis shoes of immigrants
washed up on the shores of livable geographies

I pretend disinterest, turn up the radio
mimicking those people
wishing for a summery, blithe smile,
taking more but asking less

Anniversary Poem III

Nesting nightjars in pixelated camo
beneath mums holding a place for summer,
an adjustment often mistaken for a season
Which is the way we asked and answered
while loading the dishwasher back then,
spending words like the day's cash tips
on answers we rehearsed learning
that time also isn't money,
can't be saved or wasted, a night sound
to be listened for, lifted, one thing from many

The Birthday Poem

The first time I imagine I saw it
was in the round, bulbed hubcap
of a '70 VW Squareback,
my form twigged and budded
on the chrome.
Next was a merry-go-round,
spindle wrapped with flashing,
metalflake dune buggies and fire trucks.
Then maybe the glass
of a bowling alley ice cream machine,
a glimpse on the polished surface
of a Chinese throwing star.

It stayed out of mirrors
until I thought to use them to see myself
then suddenly appeared,
a nag at my brain like a hitch in
stride or catch, breathing.

I couldn't look,
instead compromised with darkness
and various dim,
accommodatingly ineffective light fixtures.
I learned to stand back and
away, seeing and not for years.
Until what, I realized that I'm lovely?
No, nothing like that just
a recognition

that while I was avoiding the boy he
had grown quiet from
the angry, painful blemish of becoming
and now, aged into the blur,
no longer had to squint, could
even in the glare
see himself gently.

An Empathy

The fly fallen
into the goat's yellow feed bucket
had given up,
stunned by the morning frost

I watched him, aware of a residual fear
of being accidentally eaten
acquired earlier that morning
waking in the dark to
the cheery bird voices
of your wheezy breathing

which turned threatening after a while,
the way that birds can,
in too large a group or beating at the window.

So, in solidarity I slid the fly
up and out of the bucket with a careful finger

to take his chances on the ground,
filthy with mud and mouse turds

but less contemptuous of his immediate future
and returned home satisfied
that I had in mutual fashion bettered my odds
against the probability of a bite.

Cow Creek

What we called a crick,
no wider than a standing leap
one side to the other,
a rat snake stretched in pasture sun,
kinks shear as paper cuts
where the water fought to go straight.
We flipped cow patties
with pocketknives
for worms that writhed
on hooks bounced
with a neat underhand
into the water upstream
from a bend, floated
to where we imagined brook trout
sieved the current
waiting in their element
the way that the pasture bull
watched us with tiny eyes
while we walked the twisting water
among his swishing, farting cows
just this side of his allowance,
learning to mind our shadows
so as not to spook
the skeptical moment

An Epiphany

Those times the light is uncertain, forgets
to lick and mother

the shapes of the world
usually homogenous,
become brittle and brail
speaking in sharp little barks

A fluorescent second
in the grocery store maybe,
looking up from my phone and seeing you,
hair like a curtain
behind which
you're examining the contents
of a yogurt freezer

etched in ozone, up the nose,
on the backs of my eyes:
who you are and what you want;
a discerning instant before
the relief of you retreats
by quick, familiar degrees

(I remember to forget)

to the barest dimensions of distant home
that I follow, behind
and out of the way
with dissipating scratch of you
like that of a raspberry briar
on the back of my hand
long after I part it, or the air fretting
passage of a bird

Lords of Appetite

Watching a goat chew,
rows of neat and tiny teeth I wonder
about the many mouths
right now opening and closing,
a terrifying weather of hunger
at work all over the world,
and imagine a tree
alone in the very center of a great savannah
and perched at the top, us
Lords
over pigs, hawks,
feral cats, Orcas, ants, each
thing made small from the height
of our hunger
which is insatiable,
biting tit to dirt,
after which we imagine a heaven
where we will feast forever

Boys Life

A birthday party,
son of the contractor who built our small house,
his own, piecemeal and afterthought.
We discovered a garden,
fruit left to rot, and giddily tarred each other
with seedy ick, then rode home on trash bags,
skunked dogs
but feeling as if we'd glimpsed in the narrative
of the neat planting, its mysterious disregard,
and the strange approval
beneath our mother's exaggerated frustration,
what a man's life might be

Imposter Syndrome

A low bubbling in a carrying air
that continues for some time
just perceptibly becoming

until the bike and rider,
a blurred assembly,
catch enough light to be seen
and begin to grow
toward actual size, separating
into distinct parts:
bike, rider, handlebars, seat, tires

a kind of exploded view
of the relationship of each thing to the other
except that of the Softail, man
and mountain,

weight pulling against slick gravity
rider whipping the promise
of throttling the flat below,
following the sexy twist,
talking past the loose gravel
of the inevitable return, hunch

and low gear creep
of awkward mismatch:
leathers, helmet,
gleaming Harley ridiculous
in the dirt road dust,

pop and ping of skidding descent,
worse, the growl that thrummed,
snarled and toothed them
on the asphalt, now
a laugh
chaffing from the hardwoods

Game Trail

The first thing I killed
I shot because it moved

When my heart in my chest
is the tiny pink brains
of that chickadee I

find a stump in my mind,
sit and remove my socks and shoes
and run, game for the trail

of my fragile materials
silently complaining under foot, a
difference in the light, joy

of a kind chancing
my bored boy and his gun

Anthropomorphism

A notched perfect square
emptied of tenon
chiseled in a grayed post
shouldering cheap wire dog fence
cornered in your yard
inspiring dove burred sympathy
for forced retirement
of clever technique, surrender
of pull and tension
to a loose, helix'd present
that no longer sings
at every lighting bird
but rather sighs a sprung relief
at each trespass having
finally won no need
of skill other than the means
of its grain now being teased apart
by the monsoons, August
bloating and shrinking
expectations to a seasonal mean
by which I mean mine,
over half gone also or gained maybe
watching hummingbirds
at the sentiment of my invented
universal conditions
from a plastic chair.

Roosevelt Island

Is there any romance to waking up in that
blue three person, three season tent
in a patch of grass just beyond
the overpass heading into town?
Surely the occupants have had a moment,
watching the sun descend
over the T.R. Bridge, glinting
Rosslyn office glass and bounced
from the slick Potomac,
of pure animal contentment
rivaling that experienced
by any of the salaried workers
commuting between winery weekends
and eccentric Vrbos. Across the river,
two deer are grooming each other
in a Bruegel-like like snowy wood
minus the peasants
whose winter misery seems so content.

Clout Dogs

The rusty screech of the ironing board
unfolding, a kind of alarm
maybe for the newly noticed hesitance
of daylight, that wheel
having rolled back and around
quietly past the sleeping good things we keep
such as your bare legs swishing a skirt
pacing while fastening an earring,
shapely as thirty years ago
when a neighbor drawled
watching you climb my fire escape,
'That gal's got a fine behind,'
or your voice, the trailing timbre
of Texas to Virginia
still cleaving your phrases
while we maintain habit, side by side
at a cluttered sink, in the smell of blow dryer,
hair spray and deodorant,
peering at ourselves in twin mirrors,
preparing a face hoping
that we remain enough
while each thing is succeeded by another
crossing the slipstreams we make
from bathroom to dresser,
clothes selected and discarded,
phones, keys, found, inside jokes made
and tensions navigated to open the door

and go somewhere, leave
our raised and petted things behind
growling and whining, dreaming
our dreams, digesting the little shames
and failed educated guesses that satisfy them
until we return, expecting
the rush of love, tongues and noses
and the demand to be fed, which we do,
hands flat,
fingers bent away from their teeth.

Partners

I see them standing in yards
this time of year
wearing overlarge coats
and knit hats on weekends
watching partners on ladders
limbing trees or cleaning gutters.
They turn at the bass thump
of cars at the Stop sign,
think of their own
Wranglers and mini Coopers,
personality used
to a suggestive in between.
Sometimes they wave hesitantly
asking an uncertain connection
that they leave
to take on the character of its landing,
raked up years later,
a faded gesture, gorgeous because
it's forlorn and vanishing
according to its properties.

Belt

Reaching in the dark
to pull it with a shush
from where it was draped
after snicking it from a waist
the night before
with the same sound
of sliding over

A long rectangle
of cow hide cut
as you'd open a box,
the voice of changing
once or twice a day,
odds on accidentally fitting
a moment here or there
to that description

Poem that Fails to Explain
My Absence from a Family Gathering

It's difficult to remember, Sister,
looking at him now, but back then he was Zeus ...

... at dinner I brought it up, expecting sympathy.
He paused from cutting his food
and looked at me as if 'John Lennon' was a curse,
like 'God Damn' or 'Mother Fucker.'
'Good,' he said. 'That pinko commie,'
each word spit hard in my direction.
He stared at me a moment,
as if to emphasize his warning,
then abruptly continued to eat.

I didn't know what a 'pinko commie' was
but I felt that it described someone like me,
a bookish and slight boy
with the tendencies of a woman,
and doubt of his love, like backfilling dirt,
began to trickle down
onto the lid of my coffin,
the one that every child carries waiting
to have to crawl into.

Decades later, while helping me paint a barn,
he began to apologize
but I waved it away
because I knew by then I had achieved
proof beyond doubt

that I was his kind of man, no pinko commie,
my own cartoon god
of sky and thunder and was certain
that his apology
would be for misjudging my character
rather than rejecting it

though now I'm not so sure

and wish that I had let him speak
while he still had a mind to.

Rest Stop

A cluster of restaurants,
gas stations. Better
or worse depending
on the state you're in.
America, stitched ideas
of home, each dismissed
by the other as being a stop
on the way to somewhere else.

I made a lot of promises
while trying to convince you
to join my company.
I hope you feel I've kept them,
and that you consider
the people here
with a home team disdain.

This is what I'm thinking,
waiting for you to finish in the bathroom,
while watching a backpacker,
frizzy yellow hair fired
by the rising sun, begin her walk
to a good spot beside the on ramp,
a silhouette
of hope or resolve;
I'd like to know which.

Yet, the Dogs

Your forest floor beneath pine trees below
a glacial saddle, my open window, humid,
chirping night and a record player

Theme rooms

in a brutalist, modular love
that would rather assume than try,
making an ass of you and me waiting
to age out, embarrassed

poor little rich kids
clutching comfort manufactured
by other small necessities
mothering their own inventions
in less fortunate places
on assembly lines asking
cheap junk to gaze a way back

Unable to stop expecting rescue, any day
Crawling on knees offering skin
as if enough in and of them to trade

for a bespoke forgiveness
no one taught us how
to create yet, yet the dogs

are asleep and we're shoulder to shoulder, cooking in a winter kitchen,
sleet scratching at the window,
a song of distinction between need and want.

Listening to Brian Wilson in the Snow

Considering bills, arrangements,
enmities and friendships,
places of shelter and exposure while
a hatch of large, wet and awkward flakes
swarm the ineffective wipers
making a cocoon of my warm car,
Brian Wilson on the radio
asking for Love and Mercy,
an old, unfashionable song
although the snow, newborn to the season,
might argue otherwise,
like the bang and rev of a trash truck
at 4 am in a new city
recalibrating routine, the wrestling
of expected color and bleary white telling
level of change, assuming
that it forgives, will not bury me,
sitting in the driveway listening
long after the music has ended,
the faces of bearding hickories
leaned above the slushed, tinted moonroof
suggesting gods, maybe
stooped to, by, creation

Song

King of the Road

Newborn shadows jump from the reaching cedars
as the truck passes what do you see?
Anything you can imagine
No cure, yet the sun rises beneath pond ice,
above, mallards become smoke.

Dreams are mud on the belly of the pony.

A squat business park slinks by
pulling an empty parking lot behind it.
Waking up every day a person, what to do?
Stillness is death.

Halogen sunrise, flashing red beside the road
a sailor's delight, sirens gawked, lip read
from a noise canceled cabin
and following seas home,

mail dropped onto the kitchen table,
shoes removed;
nothing required between your energies
and this floor, the road of your people,
spooned miles counted in dog nail clicks,
the chain of events.

Cruising that loop,

trying to out-pace the jacked up, bored out,
candy apple dignities stroking and roaring,
one arm draped on the wheel as if you don't care

and the other

shawling the softening shoulder of love
while the now aged shadows climb
back into the trees
to sleep above their rowdy wake.

The Art Thief

She chased me down, caught me at an intersection, ran behind the car and recorded my plate on a white shopping bag which I thought was maybe from Baked & Wired, or a card shop, card shops I thought, also use those sturdy white bags, but the image of her gray head bent over the squashed bag, paling Eisenhower Building in the background, Potomac sky, 102 in August, etc.; what is called an indelible image, fled with from the scene after she strode around the car to rap the window convinced I had wronged her and I mumbled a denial unconvinced I had not, failing our interaction the same way that I failed my SATs, turning questions of fact into philosophy and so sped away when the light turned green while she shrunk in the rearview blocking E Street looking for the damage she was certain she'd accrued, thinking I'd escaped, which I had, but not with the thing she suspected me of stealing.

Tasseography

My old man would say, "knock on wood"
and I'd scoff, "age and superstition"
but now, rolled apart,
propped on an elbow
reading the streaks of brunette
in the drained cup of your hair, well,

no one tells you about the twilight
how important it is to seeing
the softness of being
between one thing and another, how

luck floats the dregs, penumbra,
light begged and teased
from the murk of promises and expectations;
cycling opaque bodies shadowing
our lover's clarity now

affecting carelessness, gesturing,
catching the ash
in tea callused hands.

Clovis

Hickory leaves, broad and knapped
as a Clovis point, caught and kept
in the ribs of the dirt road,
buried by degrees and season,
newer nearly white, older taking
more of the color of the clay, others
like the dark suggestions of bottom fish
yet all varnished in afternoon light
so that what I think of is decoupage,
tomb art taught to school children,
and how practical to know that skill
while inhabiting time, the pleasures
of which are these little sacrifices
of purpose and productivity
to the benevolent god of idle curiosity

The Evidence Suggests

an early storm
goldenrod recovering at an angle,
road speaking in a damp whisper
Walking the dog
thinking about Donald Hall,
the Names of Horses,
mine unwritten,
what they would have taken or left
refusing every debt,
reserving the willingness to spectacularly suicide
If I spell them out they'll stay,
won't return for curiosity or food
Untouchable, not by violence
or care nothing
to do with my love
but reflect it back substance-less
as the bodies the dog conjures
from wet bits of leaf and scat,
halting us for minutes
to suss the motivations of each consciousness,
not satisfied to coexist without
the optimism
that their shape requires her nose

Psalm

Twisted 'round a finger
a pluck and tie
recalling technique and rhyme,
mama had a baby and its head popped off,
in on the joke, now
grass gone to seed
able to perceive
the gluey, shark skinned fibers
of closely held futures
and fling them
with a flick and song describing
the mechanics of a laugh

Fire Drill

There is an aspect of carnival to every emergency,
an exciting release from routine milling around,
waiting on novelty, expecting the arrival
of the unforeseen thing.
Even the construction site across the street,
a scene of daily bang and turn,
is expectant, wondering,
hard hats tilted at rest, in Spanish or Portuguese.
Bomb threat? Active shooter? Fire maybe,
still remembered as a thing that can happen,
likelihood diminished by the increased odds
of a more targeted brutality while we,
the disgorged, shoot the shit,
remember whose spouse has a new job
or who has recently moved, practicing
the kind of calculated friendliness that perforates
the outlines of our one-dimensional relationships
until the all clear is given and we migrate
to wait for the escalators packed to move
maximum product back to offices and cubes,
chairs that tense to bear our weight
put to the work we are paid for
having proved that if necessary,
despite the contrary evidence of our spent time,
we can orderly save our own lives
while the hammering of the alarm squats deep
in the dark of our ears,
head cocked toward the light
and the floor wardens put away their clip boards,
relics of a time before the middle class doubted
that names were dear and heads counted

Low Water

No matter how slowly you drive, the dirt road
kicks and cries out, agitates in your wake
until you hit state-maintained asphalt
where there's a crow eating a Cheeto
on the yellow line
and cars crowd the boat launch,
people and plastic silting the drought tamed river

The time of year,
that you keep your mouth closed in the shallows
or you'll ride home
with an incubating case of the shits,
though it's difficult to believe that of the water,
wet haired and smooth shouldered beyond
the bikini pinched women chasing toddlers, men
beer stoned in lawn chairs, the weekend masses
navigating diapers, paper plates,
tangles of monofilament
to wade into summer relief and
passing over the low water bridge you believe
what the river knows
and we say but don't trust; that we are
each one and the same, dust
settling, ineffective topsoil,
a loose lifetime per inch of us, run off
without a thought come next high water

Please Share

A plea thought socially acceptable
even by those who have never
and wouldn't solicit anyone
for anything no matter the cost,
never anticipate the reward
of another's generosity yet
post without a cringe
this polite hope
that a door will open to those who knock
and behind it
a place you've never been, couldn't afford,
not with money nor the fit of you,
an awkward shape
that you've never been certain
how to fold yourself into
yet desire despite
the discomfort portended
by the known differences
in dimension between the hurt
that roughs you up, sexy and rabbiting,
and the fiddlehead longing
to unfurl in a world with no teeth.

Trash

"What kind of person,"
I asked the dog watching from the 4 wheeler
as I cleaned up Styrofoam,
spilled onto the leaves beside the road,
split trash bag like an empty stomach.

When a truck crunched past
I wondered was it them,
imagining their shame,
a stranger forced to navigate
the loose shoulder of their carelessness

and nearly fell, righting myself
on a slick young sumac
that chastised me, somehow,
with the image of each mess I've made and fled,
and rarely with the kindness
to burden a stranger.

Let Me Be There

Maybe the question isn't, do insects feel pain,
but rather are we able
to leave them to whatever it is that pleases them
by whatever means they derive pleasures
loud with love for the soft, dry bedding of habit
like the hollow bouncing clunk
of my coffee cup meeting
the porcelain of the sink,
a sound that seems to me to convey
all the care I am able to carry knowing
I've set a limit so as to be able to bear it
as no god is willing to step in, give us a break
from the repeatable outcomes of destruction.

If we can, then why not be better deities
of care breathing,
like the long dead star broadcasting
from nostalgia,
our only known afterlife,
Let Me Be There
for the spider crouched behind the record player
harming nothing, one of a trillion things
over which we might make a difference
if we considered them siblings of our joy.

Enucleation

Poached
is what I think,
every time,
yolk spooned
from a neat bowl of bone
which seems,
crazily,
improved, prepared
for some further sight:
a hagstone, a hazelnut, an egg
guessing more
than the thief
rattling in a nearby tree,
full of the past
or buzzards riding the warmth
of what they assume
is the future
above the still, eyeless
present.

Bees

There must have been scouts,
twos and threes nosing around
for a whiff of familiar collective memory
but I forgot those
camouflaged in gravel, barn wood.
Bees are always in the clover,
hanging around the stock tank
but never a mood of bees
where there had been air, a swirling ball
coating the horses stomping flies.

We swam them that summer,
a flood on the paddock.
At height of day
they disappeared to cool their queen.
Thousands of wings
beneath the floor
humming our unused space
fading into afternoon chores.
Near dusk they one by one returned to sleep.
It was a crazy harmony,
all of us dragging the harrows,
swinging the hammers,
carrying faith to being
chaff airborne shadowing
our seeds on the ground.

Urinal Poem

Those with pitted chrome, mold in the caulk,

in places of natural fraternity and exposure
such as locker rooms, pools,
truck stops, bath houses
where the line between man
and boy is thinnest,
permeable,
where your father's
or grandfather's trunk and tangle
sways unabashedly,
expectations momentarily hung
reasonable, measured.

Not those off-gassing new construction,
slick as Teflon,
bragging their glazing,
no cakes disintegrating
to pink film in chips, stains, rust,
just gleaming chrome
distorting my reflection
instead of tuning me up
the way that old porcelain will do,
giving me back to myself
like this feed store urinal
endowing me
with the stubborn DNA

of the men who stood before me undone
reaching into work stained Carhartts
and then settling down into their guts,
stirring mine as I splash it's
not day, or night
or any hour or minute --
possibly another plane
of existence altogether, one in which I am
thankfully

momentary relived
of every individual need

Hillbilly

We would roll down every hill,
home up our noses in the grass and dirt,
no different than the voles or woodchucks,
rats nesting beneath the chicken coop,
creatures of a landform,
as if the hills were separated by sea
from a mainland,
nothing walked up or in
but created as a unique species
which at times I've conceited, all of us here
having adapted in uncommon ways
though we're usual
as the carp lunking in the muddy spring,
whose enduring intelligence for survival blooms
patient as the grainy, gangly
resemblances treed on our walls
above barking story,
a regional game, training
the myth of ourselves, irresistible as
a ride hitched on flattening forces,
hip catching on the horizon then giving way
above a hollow
coaxing your particular shape
to its fertile ordinary.

Towel

Your towel, smelling of you
in the moment that you sling
the curtain of the shower back, a
shudder and metallic hiss like an
air brake release
to stand reaching a hand
blinking water from your eyes
pink and rubbery
as if wearing a child's suit of skin
hair flat and tangled
and for a moment dyed dark all
of you walked forward back
into time, one towel
around your middle, one
around your head, dressed for
barefoot travel.

Hanging, your towel
reminds me of handing it to you,
that moment when the weight of it
is relieved,
which has been your gift to me,
an appreciation of lightness, like
steam, mornings
when the nocturnal river
is late back to bed,
its breath still soaking every valley,
each desire
grazing the quench
before the sun burns it away.

Commuter Culture

Normally, roadkill has the decency
to either flatten into unrecognizable trash
or rest in a kind of taxidermic pose
resembling the activities of its life
but this deer was not graced
with that kind of death, nor
any afterlife I can imagine,
her head stretched neatly across the double line,
neck trailing off into spinal column and nerves
as if abruptly unplugged from her body,

a bio-tech horror striking me
with the idea that she could be a person
easily, they all could,
littering our asphalt
in various states of agony and decomposition,
and we wouldn't look twice, not unless
they were splayed in a
spectacular, memorable fashion
and then maybe we'd briefly wonder
at the mystery of ourselves
before shifting, merging
into the flow of maybe blessed,
certainly brutal, adaptability,
our harvest of invention
in the ignored rearview receding

The Third Law of Motivation

Mossed rocks
skidded into place over time
brakes
beneath a show of reckless descent

Never young for us,
only pretending

a lifetime rarely used
for its intended purpose
often lost
to rust in high, wet, grass
while anything willing
is leant
the weight of what's at hand

Plain
in a Joe-Pye'd clever trap
of effort
passed hand to hand

Water
neither created nor destroyed,
proof that persistence
is the less resistant path

Anniversary Poem II

Remember the tracked snow?
It was last to melt
and so was like a suture
in the flattened grass,
Robins feeding
impression to impression,
hashes as if marking time passed
from The Incident
that dried the trees,
brooded a generation of change
in their damped, stubborn ashes

& then, as if voicing that fire,
The Crack
of a stick giving to your weight
panicked the Robins.
We watched them scatter,
black thrown seeds,
the press of your taut belly
a hard pressure at both of our spines

We felt it then, but never said,
how love, like snow, is a tension
between transition
and the late present
misremembered as stillness

By now it goes without saying,
all of the lessons
to short, illogical ends
we've hefted and carried
from forest to meadow and back

Consider the Day

Thousands of mosquito larvae
wiggle beneath the glass of surface tension spotted with
locust petals
slowly spinning, coming to rest
against water lettuce hiding fat,
frowning goldfish
scales like hot, strange alloys.

A puddle from the perspective of the locust, swaying
A spot to the heron dragging its feet, light stooping

to move its shadow from the rocks before settling on a
description, the flocking face of intelligence
orienteering toward a suggested shape;

you,

a striped summer chaise, holiday for
the tired, sweating sun,
standing by the pond wearing the hour
and considering a droppered vial of insecticide
like eardrops decades ago
warmed in a soup pan,
dragonfly blue bobbing glass

a daydream
also smelling of vegetable heat
and in it rain like
a whiff of dead cloud-animal
beneath the bougainvillea.

Acknowledgements

Thank you to the editors and readers of the journals and magazines that first housed the poems in *Cicada, Dog & Song*, including: *Ablanatha Journal, Crow Step Journal, Slab Magazine, Cleaver Magazine, Cacti Fur, The City Key, High Horse, Common House Magazine, Catalogue Magazine, The Broken Plate, North of Oxford, The Thieving Magpie, Milk House Review, Temz Review, Susurrus Magazine, Halfway Down the Stairs, Dreich Magazine, Brief Wilderness, Reformed Journal, Pinhole Poetry,* and *the engine(idling)*.

Thanks to Michelle, my spouse, partner and best friend, whose picture, to quote Jason Isbell, was always in my mind, and whose presence makes my home. Thanks to Autumn, my daughter and fellow poet, who I also imagined decades before we met.

Thank you to poet Chip Miller who, thirty years after thinking he had done all he could for me, agreed to become my teacher again. Thank you to Virginia Woolf for *To The Lighthouse* and Marilynne Robinson for *Housekeeping*, books that root all my poetry, and to Dr. Dana Heller who introduced me to both. Thanks to our current dogs, Danny and Scarlett, who appear in several of these poems. Thanks to Julien Baker for the stunning, soul stirring rendition of *Claws In Your Back* with the National Symphony Orchestra that inspired the poem 'At The Kennedy.'

Thank you to the Latin American and Mexican cultures that have gifted such richness to our lives in the US, including *milagros*.

Thanks lastly to the beautiful places I call home: DC, the Shenandoah Valley of Virginia, Traverse City, Marquette, San Diego, San Bernardino, and Philadelphia.

THE AUTHOR

Matt Thomas is a smallholder farmer, engineer, and poet. *Cicada, Dog & Song* is his second full-length collection. His first, *Disappearing by the Math*, was published in 2024 by Silver Bow. A chapbook, *Foxy Love: All-American Poems,* will be published by Kelsay Books in 2026.

His poetry has appeared in *Triggerfish Critical Review, Ponder Review, Hampden-Sydney Review, Hiram Review, Dunes Review, Avalon Literary Review, Galway Review, Milk House Review, Cleaver Magazine, River Heron Review, The Thieving Magpie, Common House Magazine, Slab Magazine, The Broken Plate, Spellbinder Magazine, Pinhole Poetry, Susurrus Magazine, Temz Review, Broken Tribe Review, Serving House Journal,* and elsewhere.

He and his family live in Virginia where they practice land conservation and stewardship in the historic Shenandoah Valley. They are glad denizens of DC, Philadelphia, Traverse City, Marquette, San Diego, and San Bernardino.

www.mattthomaspoetry.com

www.ingramcontent.com/pod-product-compliance
Lightning Source LLC
Chambersburg PA
CBHW060535080526
44586CB00012B/737